The Wild West in American History

TRAILBLAZERS

Written by Harriet Upton
Illustrated by Luciano Lazzarino
Edited by Arlene C. Rourke

Library of Congress Cataloging-in-Publication Data

Upton, Harriet, 1945-
   Trailblazers.
      p.   cm. —(The Wild West in American history)
   Summary: Describes the exploits of men who explored the
American West during the early 1800s, including Lewis and Clark,
John Colter, Joe Walker, and Thomas Nuttall.
   1. West (U.S.)—Description and travel—To 1848—Juvenile
literature. 2. Explorers—West (U.S.)—History—Juvenile
literature. 3. United States—Exploring expeditions—Juvenile
literature. [1. West (U.S.)—Discovery and exploration. 2. Ex-
plorers. 3. United States—Exploring expeditions.] I. Title.
II. Series.
F592.U67 1990
978′.01   89-6141
                                                       CIP
   ISBN 0-86625-369-6   AC

Rourke Publications, Inc.
Vero Beach, Florida 32964

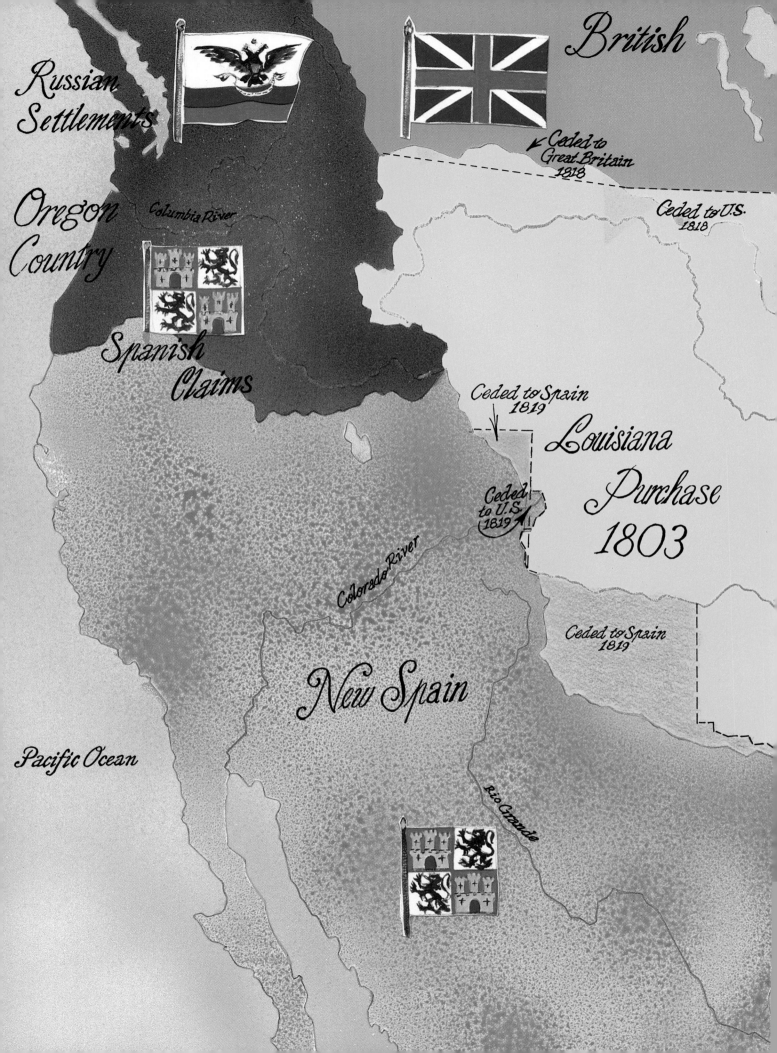

North America
TRAILBLAZERS

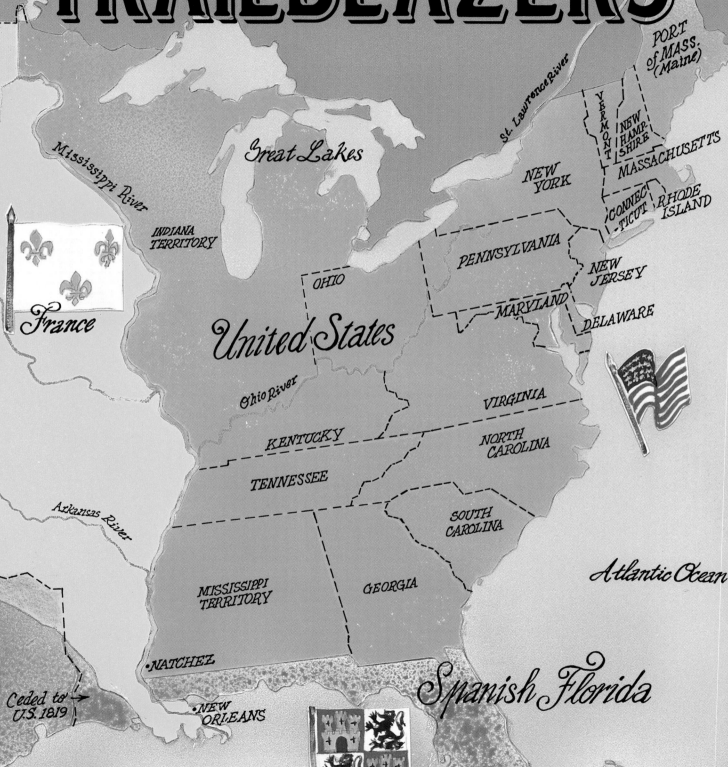

Great Lakes

St. Lawrence River

PORT of MASS. (Maine)

VERMONT

NEW HAMP-SHIRE

Mississippi River

NEW YORK

MASSACHUSETTS

INDIANA TERRITORY

CONNEC-TICUT

RHODE ISLAND

France

OHIO

PENNSYLVANIA

NEW JERSEY

United States

MARYLAND

DELAWARE

Ohio River

VIRGINIA

KENTUCKY

NORTH CAROLINA

TENNESSEE

Arkansas River

SOUTH CAROLINA

Atlantic Ocean

MISSISSIPPI TERRITORY

GEORGIA

Ceded to U.S. 1819

•NATCHEZ

Spanish Florida

•NEW ORLEANS

Gulf of Mexico

(Photo courtesy of Colorado Historical Society.)

TRAILBLAZERS

From the moment the North American continent was discovered, the West has held a unique attraction for some people. In the early days, "the West" meant Niagara Falls, in what is now western New York State. Later, the frontier pushed west to Ohio and Kentucky, and then to Missouri.

In the late 1700s, such explorers as Daniel Boone helped in this westward expansion. Boone led people on the Wilderness Road from North Carolina and Virginia through the Cumberland Pass to Kentucky. Once pioneers were able to cross the Appalachian Mountains, they pushed west to the Mississippi River. There, where the Mississippi meets the Missouri River, the town of St. Louis sprung up. On the edge of civilization, St. Louis became the gateway to the Wild West.

Most of the discovery of the Far West took place during the first thirty years of the nineteenth century, from the early 1800s to the 1830s. Some explorers were sent by the newly formed government of the United States to map land and begin settle-ments. Others were sent by private fur-trading companies who saw the chance to make a fortune by expanding west.

These early white explorers were not the first to have set foot on the land, and they often depended on trails made by buffalo herds or Indians. For years, herds of buffalo had sought out the easiest travel routes over mountains and across rivers. Although Indian trails sometimes followed the buffalo trails, they were often shorter and more direct.

Early trailblazers left their names in many places along the way—at Pike's Peak, Lewis and Clark Pass, Fort Bridger, Walker Lake, and numerous points in between. These men, and many others like them, ventured into uncharted, unknown territory. Because of their discoveries, later travelers were able to follow established routes. From the 1840s through the 1860s, close to a million emigrants streamed west on the Oregon Trail, the Santa Fe Trail, the Mormon Trail, and other routes west.

EARLY EXPLORERS

*I*n 1540, eighty years before the Pilgrims landed at Plymouth Rock, Francisco Vasques de Coronado began an expedition that would take him north from New Spain (now Mexico) all the way into the land that is today known as Kansas. Although he was not the first Spanish explorer to have ventured north beyond the lands held by Spain, he was the first to have traveled that far. He was looking for the fabled cities of gold that an earlier Spanish explorer had recounted. Coronado never found them because they didn't exist.

By the late 1700s, Spanish missions dotted the California coast from San Diego to San Francisco. Until 1774, all of the missionaries had arrived by ship. In that year, however, Juan Bautista de Anza succeeded in journeying by land from New Spain; he became the first non-Indian to enter California from the west.

Spanish missions thrived in California in the late 1700s.

Captain Robert Gray discoverer of the Columbia River.
(Photo courtesy of Oregon Historical Society.)

Spanish and British ships, coming around the tip of South America or west from the Philippines, had been landing at points along the California coastline since the 1500s and 1600s. Nevertheless, it was not until the late 1700s that any ships ventured farther up the Pacific coast.

In 1778, James Cook, an Englishman, sailed up the coast from California to what is now Alaska. There he and his crew found other white men, Russian traders who had come across on a northern route and were running a fur trading post. They had developed a profitable business with the Indians, exchanging European-made goods for fur pelts.

A few years later, British navigator George Vancouver (for whom Vancouver and Vancouver Island are named) and American navigator Robert Gray both explored the Northwest Coast, arriving from the west by ship. Captain Gray, who represented the Boston Marine Association, discovered the mouth of the Columbia River, which he named after his ship. That discovery secured for the U.S. claim to the land through which the Columbia flowed, including what is today Oregon, Washington, and Idaho.

In 1793, Alexander Mackenzie became the first non-native to cross the continent when he traveled on land across Canada from the Atlantic to the Pacific. Mackenzie, a Scottish fur trader, proved that it was indeed possible for people to make that overland trip safely, and he set the stage for others to follow.

Meanwhile, France had secured from Spain the rights to the Louisiana Territory, which stretched from the mouth of the Mississippi River all the way up to what is now Canada. Without knowing what the land was like, or even what its exact borders were, President Thomas Jefferson arranged to buy the Louisiana Territory from Napoleon, the French emperor, in 1803. This was the famous Louisiana Purchase, and soon afterwards, Jefferson sent Meriwether Lewis and William Clark to explore this new American territory.

Sacajawea, a Shoshone Indian, was just a teenager when she led Lewis and Clark through the Northwest Territory. Her infant son, Jean Baptiste, went on the expedition.
(Photo courtesy of Wyoming State Archives.)

Meriwether Lewis and William Clark.
(Photos courtesy of State Historical Society of Missouri.)

THE LEWIS AND CLARK EXPEDITION

Captain Meriwether Lewis was a young Army officer, a family friend of the Jeffersons who had worked as President Jefferson's private secretary in Washington. When Jefferson was ready to examine the lands acquired in the Louisiana Purchase, he told Lewis to put an expedition together.

Lewis chose William Clark as his co-commander. Lewis had served under Clark in the army, and both men had frontier experience. In preparation for the trip Lewis had studied celestial navigation, botany, anatomy, and medicine at the University of Pennsylvania and at the American Philosophical Society.

Lewis and Clark gathered the troops and equipment needed for their Corps of Discovery.

They selected experienced soldiers as well as new enlistees, and took along an Indian interpreter. Their supplies included food, tools, arms, medicines, and a collapsible canoe. They also took gifts—beads, calico, ribbons, kettles, mirrors, and more—for the Indians they would encounter.

The Corps of Discovery left St. Louis, Missouri, where the Missouri River joins the Mississippi, on May 14, 1804. They journeyed by barge up the Missouri. Their mission, as set forth by President Jefferson, was to report on what they saw, and they were instructed to take careful notes about the geography of the land as well as about the appearance and customs of the Indian tribes they encountered. Jefferson hoped that Lewis and Clark would discover a Northwest Passage—a path by water leading all the way to the Pacific coast. No one knew then if such a route existed; today we know that one does not.

In August, four and a half months into the expedition, one of the Corpsmen, Sergeant Charles Floyd, took sick and died suddenly. He was buried on a bluff near the banks of the Missouri. His gravesite is located near Sioux City, Iowa, and on it stands Floyd's Monument, a

CANADA

the EXPEDITION

Columbia R.

Marias R.

BITTER ROOT RANGE

Travellers Rest

COLUMBIA VALLEY

Canoe camp

Great Falls Mon.

Clatsop winter Quarters 1805-1806

Three Forks Camp

Yellow Stone R.

Snake R.

ROCKY MTS.

(WY

Great Salt Lake

(Utah)

Green R.

The Shoshoni Guide
Princess Sacajawea

PACIFIC OCEAN

EXPEDITION

Area Covered by the Map

Columbia River Valley

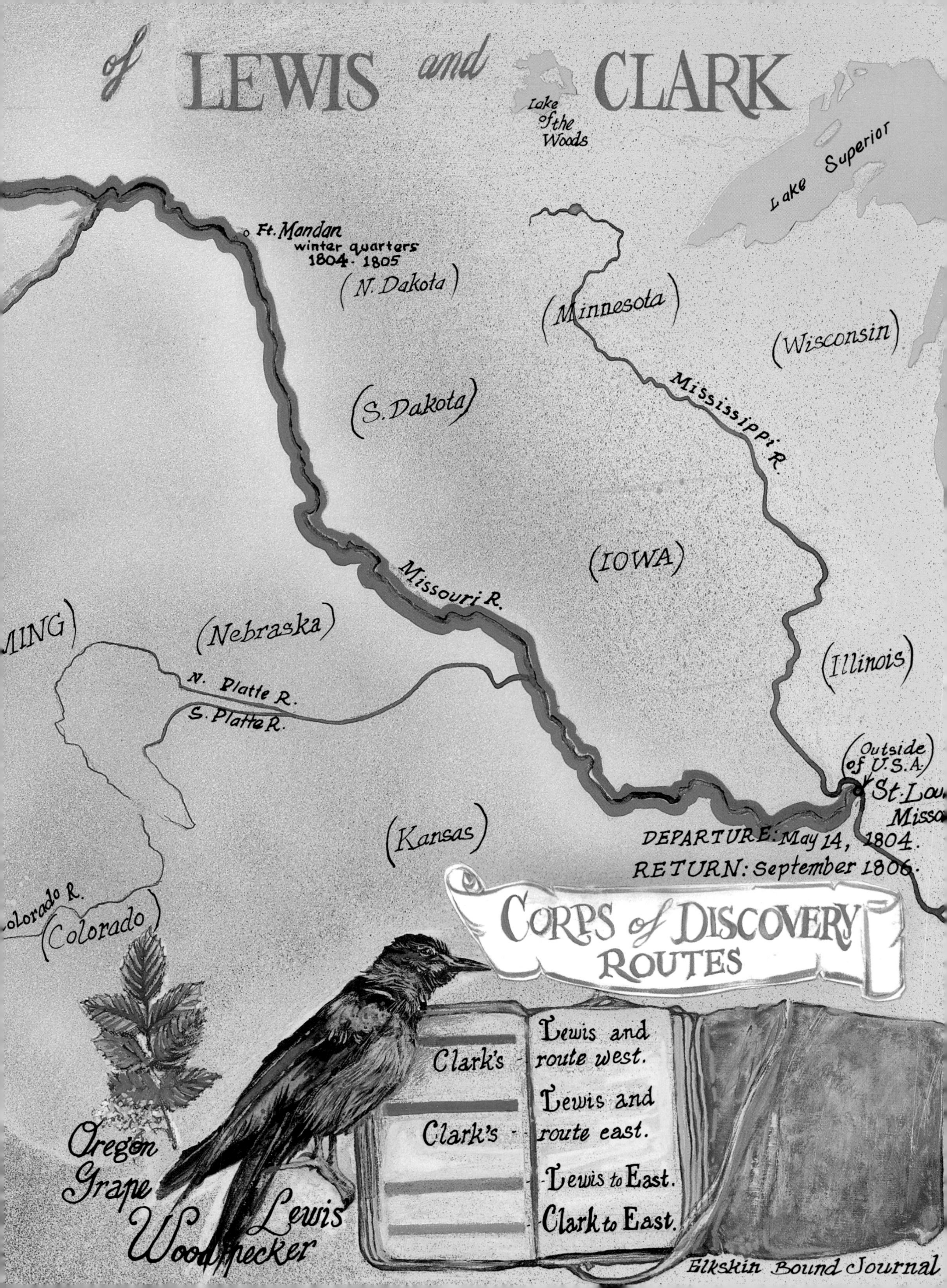

of LEWIS and CLARK

Lake of the Woods

Lake Superior

o Ft. Mandan
winter quarters
1804-1805
(N. Dakota)

(S. Dakota)

(Minnesota)

(Wisconsin)

Mississippi R.

(IOWA)

Missouri R.

(Illinois)

MING)

(Nebraska)

N. Platte R.
S. Platte R.

Colorado R.
(Colorado)

(Kansas)

(Outside
of U.S.A.)
St. Lou
Misso

DEPARTURE: May 14, 1804
RETURN: September 1806

CORPS of DISCOVERY
ROUTES

Oregon
Grape

Lewis
Woodpecker

Clark's — Lewis and
route west.

Clark's — Lewis and
route east.

— Lewis to East.

Clark to East.

Elkskin Bound Journal

National Historic Landmark.

As Lewis and Clark continued their journey north on the Missouri River, they began to encounter the Sioux tribes they had heard tales of. The first Sioux Indians they met were Yanktons, who turned out to be very friendly. Next they met the Teton Sioux, whose appearance and great numbers intimidated the explorers. Lewis and Clark stood firm, and without bloodshed they convinced the Teton Sioux to back down. From then on, the expedition was treated with respect by the natives, as word passed from one tribe to the next.

By October, the Corps of Discovery had reached the site of the Mandan Indians, near what is today Bismarck, North Dakota, and they decided to camp there for the winter. They built Fort Mandan as temporary lodging. While they were there, they met French and English fur traders who had come down from Canada to trade with the Mandans. It was here also that Lewis and Clark met Sacajawea. She was a Shoshone princess who had been taken from her people when she was young. Now, she was the wife of a Frenchman, Touissant Charbonneau, whom Lewis and Clark hired as a translator. Their infant son, Baptiste, also became part of the expedition.

The following spring, in April 1805, Lewis and Clark broke camp. They sent a contingent of men back to St. Louis in a barge to report on their progress to date, and the rest of the Corps of Discovery continued up the Missouri River in eight canoes. This leg of the trip was more difficult than the previous one; at one point a storm overturned one of the canoes. Fortunately, no one was injured, and most of the supplies were salvaged.

At one point, they came to a fork in the river—should they take the upper or lower stream? After scouting upstream both branches, they chose the lower stream, which turned out to be the right choice. It took them to the Falls of the Missouri, a series of five magnificent waterfalls. There they were forced to travel sixteen miles by land around the falls, carrying their boats and supplies on a makeshift cart built on the spot.

Once back in the water, they experienced fast currents, bad weather, and a stream that was often dangerously narrow. At the end of July they came to the Three Forks, where the Jefferson, Gallatin, and Madison Rivers join to form the Missouri. They poled up the Jefferson River, which was becoming narrower and more shallow. Sacajawea began to recognize the land from her Shoshone childhood. At the head of the stream, when they could go no farther by boat, they hid anything they did not absolutely need, and they set off by foot toward a pass in the mountains. Sacajawea remembered that it led to the homes of her people.

Soon, they encountered their first Shoshone Indian, who fled without talking to them. Following him, they discovered a trail that took them through the pass (now named Lemhi Pass) to the other side of the Continental Divide. There they met up with other Shoshones, who invited Lewis to their camp. When Sacajawea arrived at camp, she was overjoyed to see people she knew, including her brother, who was now the tribe's chief.

When the Corps of Discovery was ready to continue their journey to the Pacific, the Shoshones sold them as many horses as they could spare and supplied them with a guide. The expedition traversed the mountainous terrain under difficult circumstances—snow, wind, and harsh weather. They could find little to eat along the way, and the men were weak, hungry, and often sick.

Finally, in September, the Corps of Discovery staggered into a Nez Perce village at the foot of the Bitterroot Mountains. The Nez Perce were friendly, and they helped the men build canoes to continue their journey. Soon the expedition was afloat down the Clearwater River, which flowed into the Snake River and then into the Columbia River. On November 7, 1805, they reached the headwaters of the Columbia River; from there, it was just a few miles to the Pacific Ocean. They built a winter camp, which they named Fort Clatsop after a local Indian tribe.

Lewis and Clark's journey from St. Louis to the Pacific Ocean had taken almost eighteen months. Their return trip took just six months. They followed the same route as far as Lolo Pass, where they crossed the Bitterroot Mountains. Then they split up, with Clark and one group taking the southern route by land down to the Yellowstone River and then traveling by water on the Yellowstone to the Missouri River. Lewis took the northern route where he explored the Marias River—the fork they didn't take on their trip out—and traveled on the Missouri River to the spot where it joined the Yellowstone. There Lewis and Clark met up again and concluded their historic journey, arriving back in St. Louis on September 23, 1806.

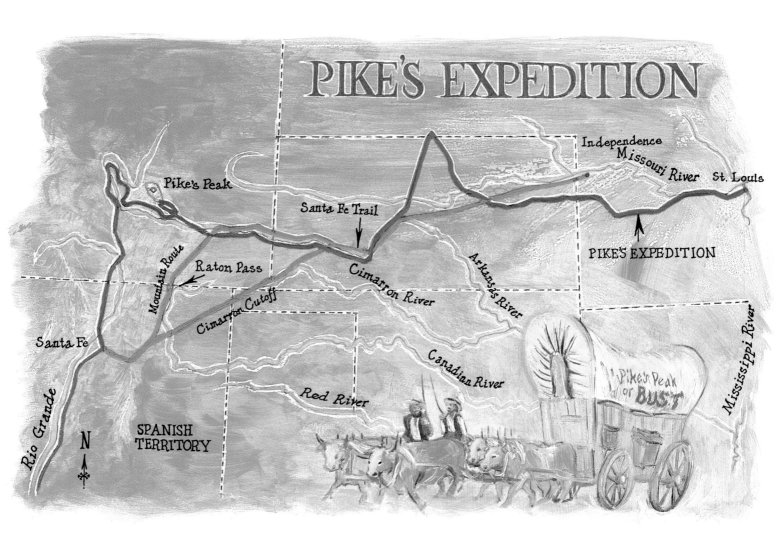

PIKE'S EXPEDITION

PIKE'S PEAK

*E*ven before Lewis and Clark arrived back in St. Louis, a young Army lieutenant, Zebulon Pike, was sent to explore the southern part of the Louisiana Purchase. His trip was grounded in politics, although he may not have been fully aware of that fact. Jefferson had just appointed General James Wilkinson governor of the Louisiana Territory, and Wilkinson was conspiring with Jefferson's rival, Aaron Burr, to set up an independent nation in the Southwest. Pike was sent

on a military mission to find out how strongly held the Spanish Territory was.

In July 1806, Pike left St. Louis by boat, traveling up the Missouri to the Osage River, and then west on the Osage past the villages of the Osage Indians. He continued his trip by land, traveling north to the Pawnee village near what is today the Kansas-Nebraska border. At this point, he sent a junior lieutenant back to Governor Wilkinson with his reports, and Pike and his men headed south toward the Arkansas River. They followed the river up to the Rocky Mountains into what is today Colorado, exploring the mountains. They sighted the mountain that was later named Pike's Peak, but it proved to be too far away and too high to scale. Strangely enough, Zebulon Pike never actually climbed the peak that was named after him.

As he pushed south, Pike and his men were arrested by the Spanish, who claimed that Pike's party had crossed into Spanish Territory. Whether he entered the Spanish Territory intentionally or was simply lost in his quest for the

Zebulon Pike.   **Major Stephen H. Long.**

source of the Red River, as he stated, will never be known. His capture and escort to Santa Fe and on to Chihuahua, Mexico (then called New Spain) for interrogation gave him an opportunity to see and learn a great deal about the Spanish Territory. The Mexican governor decided to let Pike go, and had him escorted back to the United States border near Natchitoches, Louisiana. "Language cannot express the gaity of my heart," he wrote, "when I once more beheld the standard of my country waved aloft."

Pike had painted the Great Plains as the "Great American Desert," and this description was reinforced by Major Stephen H. Long, who led an expedition through some of the same terrain in 1819-1820. Long's mission was two-fold: to survey the land and find the source of the Arkansas, Platte, and Red Rivers, and to display U.S. presence in the northern part of the territory where the British were encroaching. Long did not succeed in finding the headwaters of the rivers. Even so, he succeeded where Pike had failed—Major Long was the first white man to climb Pike's Peak.

The map Long produced in 1821 was the most accurate reflection of the land to date, but his reaction to the land was bleak. "In regard to this extensive section of the country," Long wrote, "I do not hesitate in giving the opinion that it is almost wholly unfit for cultivation, and of course, uninhabitable by a people depending upon agriculture for their subsistence."

THE SANTA FE TRAIL

*I*t is likely that the route along which the Spanish military escorted Zebulon Pike was the Santa Fe Trail. It was an old trail that had been used for centuries, first by Indians and then by the Spanish. Coronado's expedition probably traveled along part of it while heading for Kansas.

During the mid-1700s, several French traders found their way down to Santa Fe along the Santa Fe Trail. In 1804, a businessman from Illinois sent Jean Baptiste La Lande there with goods to sell. The businessman's trust was misplaced. La Lande sold the goods—but he kept the money and stayed in New Mexico.

Santa Fe remained a Spanish territory until 1821, when Mexico achieved independence from Spain. Although the Mexicans were eager to buy goods, Spanish law prohibited Americans from doing business there. Most of the Americans who tried were arrested by the Spanish cavalry, and some were even imprisoned. Mexico's independence brought a change in these laws, and many American merchants and traders were eager to take advantage of these new opportunities.

The Santa Fe Trail provided the connection between these new markets and the United States. It was over eight hundred miles long, crossing western Missouri and Kansas. Along the route were Fort Osage (later called Fort Clark) and Fort Leavenworth, built in 1827. Later, more military forts would be built to protect travelers and wage war against the Indians. The trail followed the Arkansas River through Kansas,

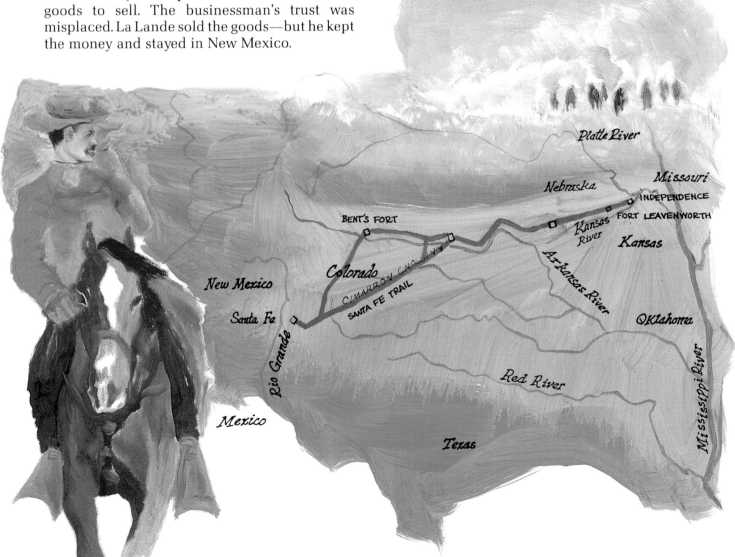

crossing prairie and then plains.

At Pawnee Rock, still in Kansas, travelers stopped to carve their names in the sandstone. Not quite a hundred miles farther, the trail split in two. One fork dropped south, leading across the Cimarron Desert to the Cimarron River and then west into New Mexico. The other fork followed the Arkansas River west into the Rockies to Bent's Fort and then turned south. The trail entered New Mexico through the Raton Pass and then rejoined the Cimarron Trail. Neither route was easy.

In 1822, Captain William Becknell left Missouri for Santa Fe with three wagons filled with goods. Becknell knew it would be difficult to pull heavy wagons over the rugged mountain pass, and so he opted for the southern route. He had underestimated the desert's scorching heat, however, and he and his men lost their way for two days, searching for water but seeing only mirages. They finally found the Cimarron River. When they reached Santa Fe, their trip marked the first time the trail had been used for non-Indian commercial trade. His trip earned Bucknell the title "father of the Santa Fe Trail."

Between 1822 and 1843, merchandise valued at millions of dollars was carried on the Santa Fe Trail. As trade along the route increased, so did the incidence of Indian hostility. In 1825, Senator Thomas Hart Benton of Missouri, the leading proponent of westward expansionism, introduced a bill in Congress to aid in achieving peace with the Indians along the route and to mark the road. Unfortunately, negotiating a peace settlement with the Osage and Kansas Indians did not solve the problem, since they were not the only tribes to bother the caravans.

In 1846, the U.S. declared war on Mexico, and, as one historian puts it, "the Santa Fe Trail became a military road." Colonel Stephen Kearny led a regiment down from Bent's Fort to Santa Fe and occupied the town. The Southwest became U.S. territory, and additional military posts were constructed along the trail. In 1848, the commander of one fort counted at least three thousand wagons passing during the summer—people moving to the West and the Southwest to build new lives.

By the late 1800s, though, the Santa Fe Trail was no longer the best means of travel. Railroads were replacing wagon trains, and in 1880, the Atchison, Topeka and Santa Fe line sent its first train into Santa Fe. That moment marked the end of the Santa Fe Trail.

THE MOUNTAIN MEN

*M*ajor fur trading companies, both those in Canada and those in colonial America, contributed greatly to the expansion of the west. Even before President Jefferson sent Lewis and Clark to explore the Pacific Northwest, representatives of the Hudson's Bay Company had ventured farther and farther west across Canada in their zeal to acquire more furs and make bigger profits. By the late 1700s, Hudson's Bay trading posts were scattered throughout the north. During his cross-country journey in 1793 to look for a Northwest Passage, Alexander Mackenzie was working for another British-owned, Canadian-based fur trader, the North-West Company.

After James Cook's report that the Russian fur traders were getting high prices for their furs in China, several Americans also decided to get in on the action. Manuel Lisa, who was actually a Spaniard but had lived in St. Louis for several years, formed a company in 1807 and set out from St. Louis up the Missouri with a band of fur trappers. En route, he ran into Lewis and Clark on their return trip and hired John Colter, who had been a member of their party.

Folks found it hard to believe John Colter's tales of geysers in Yellowstone Park.

John Colter was a true mountain man, one of many independent and intrepid trappers who explored the West during the early 1800s. They were drawn by the chance to make big money and the thrill of adventure. Some stayed because they preferred the wilderness to city life.

John Colter, a Virginian, was an experienced soldier when he was chosen to be part of Lewis and Clark's Corps of Discovery. After almost two years of traveling with the expedition in the wilderness, he had gained unique and valuable skills as a frontiersman.

During the time he worked for Manual Lisa's fur trading company, he trapped beaver and explored new areas where beaver might be found. His best known trip, taken alone in the winter of 1807-1808, was through the mountains where the states of Wyoming, Montana, and

Idaho meet. He returned with tales of incredible natural wonders—geysers, hot springs, and bubbling mudholes. Many people found it hard to believe his wild tales, and one such discovery was dubbed "Colter's Hell." Anyone today who has visited Yellowstone Park can imagine what Colter's reaction must have been, as the first white person to see such strange natural phenomenon.

William Ashley came from St. Louis. After Lisa's death, he formed the Rocky Mountain Fur Company with the intention of covering the same territory that Lisa had. Unlike Lisa, he ran into trouble with the Arikara Indians. Because of this, the river route up the Missouri to the Yellowstone and Bighorn Rivers became impossible for Ashley and his men to travel safely. Instead, he decided to see what kind of trapping and trading opportunities lay directly west, and he sent a group of men into the Rocky Mountains. Among these men were Jedediah Smith, Thomas Fitzpatrick, and William Sublette. Although they ran into serious difficulties on their trip, they managed to reach the Rockies. At the end of the trapping season, Smith and the other men stayed on to do more trapping while Fitzpatrick returned to St. Louis with the furs.

Smith and his men criss-crossed the Rockies, with no knowledge of what they would find. Now

Jim Bridger was the first white man to see the Great Salt Lake.

and then they ran into men from the Hudson's Bay Company. On later journeys, Smith traveled south from Salt Lake to Zion Canyon, across the Colorado River into what is now Nevada and Arizona, and into California. He also traveled north along the Pacific coast to Fort Vancouver and back down through the Yellowstone and Big

Horn basin areas. He was killed on an expedition to Santa Fe when he was only thirty-two, but in his lifetime had explored hundreds of miles of new territory. He is known today as one of the finest of the early explorers.

Jim Bridger and William Sublette, like the trapper/explorer Jedediah Smith, also answered Ashley's ad for "enterprising young men" and went to work for the Rocky Mountain Fur Company. During the 1825 trapping season, Jim Bridger sailed down the Bear River and ended up in the Great Salt Lake. Because the water was salty, he assumed it was connected to the Pacific Ocean. He is credited with the discovery of the Great Salt Lake, although, of course, he was just the first white man to come upon it. Bridger lived out most of his life in the West, first as a trapper, and then as a guide. William Sublette eventually became a co-owner, along with David Jackson and Jed Smith, of the Rocky Mountain Fur Company.

Yet another well-known frontiersman was lured West by the Rocky Mountain Fur Company. Kit Carson was young when he became a fur trapper, and his experiences—and many he didn't even have—were recorded in wild stories and novels published back East. His frontier skills and thorough knowledge of the land made him a trusted guide. He was one of two guides for John Fremont's expedition which was sent by the U.S. government to survey Oregon. Yet Carson is perhaps best known today for events in his later life. As a general in the U.S. Army— the Army of the West—he took part in fighting the Navajos and moving them to Bosque Redondo. Today his actions in that particular event no longer seem commendable, but at the time, he was accorded the reputation of a great Indian fighter. Carson died in 1868, the year before he would have turned sixty.

Despite all the expeditions that had explored the West—the Rockies, south to Santa Fe, and north into Oregon territory—people still knew very little about the land between the Rockies and California.

In 1833, Joe Walker was hired and financed by Benjamin Bonneville, possibly as a representative of the United States, to explore that region. California was still a part of Mexico, and most

western Wyoming, in August 1833; in choosing his route, Walker combined the sketchy bits and pieces of information gleaned from previous explorations with the knowledge of friendly Indians. Although Walker's party experienced some arduous periods, especially crossing the Sierras, they didn't lose a man, and they arrived at the edge of Yosemite Valley in November. They were the first white men to gaze on that incredible and overwhelming natural wonder. They managed to find a path to the valley floor, and then on toward the California coast. On their return trip, Walker looked for and found a pass over the Sierras that made their crossing much easier.

Joe Walker's trailblazing was crucial to the opening of the West. He had found an accessible overland route to California, and it was a route that would soon be used by hundreds and hundreds of wagon trains.

of those who had visited California had arrived there by ship. Jedediah Smith had managed to reach California by land, but his trip was a harrowing one on which many lives were lost.

Walker had plenty of trailblazing experience and was an organized and reliable leader. He assembled a party of first-rate mountain men, along with ample equipment and supplies. The expedition left Green River, in what is now

Soda Springs · Sublette's Cut Off · the OREGON TRAIL · Great Salt Lake · Fort Bridger · South Pass · Fort Laramie

THE DISCOVERY OF SOUTH PASS

John Jacob Astor was another fur trader whose business interests played a part in western expansion. In 1810 he formed the Pacific Trading Company with the goal of establishing a fort at the mouth of the Columbia River on the Pacific. To do this, he sent a party led by Wilson Price Hunt to cross the continent by land. At the same time, he sent a ship, the *Tonquin,* to sail there. The ship was laden with supplies for the new Fort Astoria. Once unloaded, it would pick up furs to take to China.

The *Tonquin*'s crew arrived first and built the fort. Somehow the ship was blown up while trading with Indians to the north. The following February, when Hunt's party began to arrive at Fort Astoria, they found an unexpectedly small welcoming committee—and no ship.

In the spring of 1813, a group representing North-West Company, backed up by the British military, arrived at Fort Astoria and demanded that the Americans surrender—Britain and the U.S. were at war. After all the hardship and all the lives lost, the Pacific Fur Company ceased to exist just three years after it was begun. Its impact on the West, however, would be significant.

In late 1812, about six months before the Pacific Fur Company surrendered to the British, a small expedition of men led by Robert Stuart set out from Astoria for St. Louis. Forced to go south to avoid meeting up with Indians, they discovered a pass through the mountains that form the Continental Divide.

South Pass, located in the southwestern corner of Wyoming, was more easily accessible than any other crossing over the mountains—the slope was gradual on both sides, and water was plentiful all along the way. They had discovered the route that later became the Oregon Trail, enabling thousands of pioneers to settle the West.

John Jacob Astor. (Photo courtesy of Oregon Historical Society.)

THE OREGON TRAIL

*I*n 1836, two missionary couples, including a medical doctor and a minister, decided to travel to Oregon to convert the Indians to Christianity. The missionaries were Dr. and Mrs. Marcus Whitman and the Rev. and Mrs. Henry Spaulding. They began their journey in wagons and ended it on foot or horseback. Their wagons stuck in the mud during river crossings and tipped over when being pulled up steep trails. Narcissa Whitman and Eliza Spaulding became the first non-native women to cross South Pass, and today the Whitman Monument near South Pass City commemorates that fact.

The Oregon Trail began in Independence, Missouri, and traveled northwest, joining the Platte River in present-day Nebraska. Along the two thousand mile trail between Independence and Oregon City were several forts and resting stations. Some were old trading posts, but most were built in the 1840s or later to protect travelers. Fort Kearny, over three hundred miles from Independence, was built in 1848 and became one of the rendezvous points for those emigrants who wanted to join a wagon train.

From Fort Kearny, it was over three hundred

more miles to Fort Laramie, located in western Wyoming. Then the trail continued for several hundred miles, passing Independence Rock, where many travelers stopped to carve their names or initials. After they crossed South Pass, it was another hundred miles to Fort Bridger. In 1843, Jim Bridger and Louis Vasquez had anticipated the needs of the emigrants and built a fort to serve them. Near Fort Hall, in present-day Idaho, the trail split. California-bound travelers went south, and Oregon-bound members continued on, crossing what is now Idaho into Oregon.

In 1841, the first true covered wagon train traversed the Oregon Trail. The Bartleson-Bidwell party, named after two of its members, was composed of emigrants bound for California and Oregon. Their guide was Tom Fitzpatrick, who had first come west in 1823 with Ashley's fur trading company. It was a very difficult journey and even though Fitzpatrick stopped the wagon train at Fort Laramie to make repairs and prepare for the rest of the trip, the wagons did not last the whole trip. The group continued on horseback, muleback, and foot. They parted ways in Idaho.

Those who went to California became its first official emigrants, arriving just ahead of another group that had taken the southern route through New Mexico. The Bartleson-Bidwell party was soon followed by other wagon trains. For those taking the Oregon Trail to California, timing was essential. The Sierras had to be crossed before the snow fell. One unfortunate party didn't make it in time.

In 1846 the Donner-Reed party left Fort Bridger to take the Hastings Cutoff down past the Great Salt Lake and across the Sierra Nevada Mountains into California. The party of eighty emigrants lost valuable time due to a detour, and a blizzard caught them in the mountain pass. Half the people in the party died; others turned to cannibalism in order to stay alive until they were rescued. The scene of their disaster in now known as Donner Pass.

In 1848, James Marshall discovered gold on John Sutter's land in California. By 1850, the Oregon Trail was full of Easterners, mostly men, with their hearts set on striking it rich. That same year, California was admitted to the Union.

Historians estimate that over 350,000 people used the Oregon Trail to move west. Not everyone was headed for California. Plenty of people were bound for Oregon, lured not by gold but land. Their final destination was Oregon City, located on the Willamette River less than fifty miles from the Pacific Ocean. Surrounding Oregon was rich farming land, and Oregon was advertised as the land of opportunity. Everyone with the courage to make the trip was promised a square mile of land, theirs for the taking.

Brigham Young led his people to the Great Salt Lake by way of the Mormon Trail.

THE MORMON TRAIL

Perhaps some of the least prepared and best prepared of all the westward emigrants were the Mormons. They were living in Nauvoo, Illinois, when they decided to migrate west to find a new home. The Mormons lived together in a community and were not always welcomed by their neighbors. That was the case in Nauvoo, where their leader and prophet Joseph Smith and his brother Hyrum were killed.

Unhappy with their living conditions, the Mormons began preparing for their journey in the fall of 1845. They built wagons and gathered supplies and equipment. In February 1846, Brigham Young left Nauvoo to lead the first group of people west. Between four and five hundred wagons set out that February, leaving Nauvoo sooner than anticipated to avoid trouble that was brewing. They had not yet decided on a final destination. They hoped to find a place that was totally unsettled, perhaps even a place that wouldn't be desirable to other people.

Crossing Iowa in the winter months proved difficult, as most travelers hadn't brought enough provisions to last more than a couple of weeks. Temperatures were consistently below the freezing point, and there was no natural grazing for the animals. In March, Brigham Young took steps to organize the traveling band, dividing it into subgroups and appointing members to be responsible for certain functions, such as buying food. In some locations where they camped, facilities were built to aid the Mormons who would follow.

The first group of Mormon emigrants arrived in Council Bluffs, on the western edge of Iowa, in June. Two factors made them decide to stay there for the year: first, the U.S. government, at war with Mexico, was asking for men to help fight; second, Mormons were still coming from Nauvoo and needed time and help in catching up. While in winter camp in Council Bluffs, the Mormons learned what they could about the route ahead.

In April 1847, a small group of less than two hundred people, called the Pioneer Company, left Council Bluffs to act as the advance party. Four to six weeks later they were followed by a larger wagon train. The Pioneer Company crossed the Platte River and journeyed along its north side. Even when they reached the point where the Oregon Trail intersected with the Platte, the Mormons decided to remain on the north side of the river and keep to themselves, rather than follow the Oregon Trail, which was on the south side.

At Fort Laramie, however, they felt it would be wiser to join the Oregon Trail, and they ferried their wagons across the North Platte. There they followed the same trail as the other emigrants, arriving at Fort Bridger in July. Finally they were faced with a decision. They could continue on the Oregon Trail, either to Oregon or California, or they could take the Hastings Cutoff, which passed the Great Salt Lake on its way to California.

The Pioneer Company had the benefit of the best advice. They had run into several people, including Jim Bridger, who knew the area around the Great Salt Lake. Young chose that direction. The trail was far less traveled and even hard to find in some spots, but they cleared it when necessary.

On July 24, 1847, Brigham Young's party arrived at the valley of the Great Salt Lake. "This is the right place," proclaimed Young. The following year, he returned to Council Bluffs to lead the second group of travelers to their new home. Historians estimate that up to 68,000 Mormon emigrants traveled to Salt Lake on the Mormon Trail. Use of the trail stopped after 1868, when the railroad replaced the wagon trail as the chief route leading west.

Fort Vancouver
Portland
Astoria   Oregon City   Oregon trail   Fort Hall   Soda Springs   Devil's Gate   Independence Rock   Mormon Trail   Nauvoo

St. Joseph
Independence
Liberty   Tipton

California Trail   Fort Bridger   Cherokee Trail   Santa Fe Trail

Sacramento
Sutters Fort   Old Spanish Trail

San Francisco   Santa Fe

Los Angeles   Oxbow Route

THE SOUTHERN ROUTE

Not everyone who arrived in California did so by ship or by following the Oregon Trail. Many emigrants came from the south, on a route that led from Santa Fe to San Diego. This trail was pioneered by Juan Bautista de Anza in 1774, long before Jedediah Smith and Joe Walker found their way there in 1827 and 1833. After that, mountain men and fur traders traveled this way, even though both New Mexico and California still belonged to Mexico.

Mountain men also found alternative routes, including one that came to be known as the Old Spanish Trail. It was considerably longer, ranging up through Colorado and down through Utah, but had the advantage of avoiding Indians. When the United States gained possession of Santa Fe in 1846, General Kearny set out to take California. Meanwhile, Lieutenant Colonel Philip Cooke and the Mormon Battalion (those men who had been recruited from Council Bluffs amid the Mormon migration) were also ordered to California from Santa Fe. They took a slightly different path, improving on Kearny's route. A year later, Major Lawrence P. Graham, took Cooke's trail but changed it somewhat. This became the southern route that subsequent travelers would use.

That was in 1848, the same year James Marshall found gold at Sutter's Mill in California. Soon the southern route, just like the Oregon Trail, was filled with hopeful forty-niners seeking their fortunes. Like the other trails west, it became rutted and worn with use.

Last Version of Fort Laramie
Remodelled in stucco

Fort Laramie
1834 - 1880's

One of the original Fort Buildings

1868
Treaty
Chief
Red Cloud

General
Sherman

Peace terms Signed at Fort Laramie

Interior View

1837 ORIGINAL Fort Laramie WOODEN STRUCTURE

THE STORY OF A FORT

*T*he early forts made a significant contribution to the opening of the West. For fur traders, they were places to meet with Indians and trappers. Later, they became welcome resting points for weary westward emigrants.

One of the most important forts was Fort Laramie, located in present-day Wyoming where the Laramie and North Platte Rivers meet. Fort Laramie was a natural stopping point along the Oregon Trail. Like many other forts, Fort Laramie began as a trading post.

In 1834, when William Sublette and Robert Campbell built the post to cater to the area's fur traders, they named it Fort William. The following year they sold it to the American Fur Company. Fort William was soon a thriving fur post and a gathering place for explorers, mountain men, fur trappers, and Indians. It was a clerk's error, according to one story, that caused the fort to become known as Fort Laramie rather than Fort William. All mail was address to "Fort William on the Laramie," but this particular clerk wrote Fort Laramie by mistake, and the name stuck.

Unlike most forts, which were built squarely north and south, Fort Laramie was built in relation to the lay of the land. It was shaped like a rectangle and built of logs. Later this building was rebuilt using adobe brick. In 1842, Fremont visited Fort Laramie on one of his mapmaking expeditions and described it in a report: "The walls are fifteen feet high surmounted with a wooden palisade and form a portion of ranges of houses, which entirely surround a yard of about 130 feet square. Every apartment has its door and window—all, of course, opening on the inside. There are two entrances opposite each other, one of which is a large and public entrance; the other smaller and more private—a sort of postern gate. Over the entrance is a square tower, with loop-holes, and, like the rest of the work, built of earth. At two of the angles [corners], and diagonally opposite each other, are large square bastions, so arranged as to sweep the four faces of the walls."

One Wyoming historian has provided fascinating details about the activity at Fort Laramie during the time it was a trading post. "Life at Fort Laramie in the early 1840s was picturesque and seldom dull. The four or five trappers who ran the post had settled down with Indian wives. Other trappers were continually coming and going. Indians made the fort and vicinity their meeting place. They came and went two or three times a year, bringing their skins to trade for beads, blankets, trinkets, tobacco, vermillion, hatchets, and steel arrowheads. They traded for ammunition and whiskey, too, if they could get them."

After 1843, Fort Laramie became a stopping place for all western emigrants. The westward expansion had begun in earnest, and the number of wagon trains coming west was increasing. The Plains Indians, across whose land the wagon trains were rolling, were not always hospitable to the travelers. People were pressing the government for protection, and in response, the government began setting up a network of forts along the Oregon Trail, the major route west.

In 1848, the U.S. government bought Fort Laramie from the American Fur Company and stationed three companies of soldiers there. Their first task was to construct new buildings, and they set to work sawing trees into lumber and collecting sand and lime so they could make concrete. At one time, Fort Laramie had as many as thirty or forty buildings. Today twenty-two of these original structures remain standing.

During the height of westward emigration, Fort Laramie was a haven for many thousands of emigrants. After weeks of arduous travel, sometimes life-threatening, they took comfort at the sight of whitewashed walls, military troops, and other wagons. Weary travelers could rest while their supplies were replenished and their wagons repaired. Fort Laramie had a blacksmith shop to fix wagon wheels and reshoe horses; the fort also stocked supplies to sell to the emigrants. The prices of goods, which had been prohibitively high when Fort Laramie was a trading post, were once again fair: six cents for a pound of sugar, two and a half cents for a pound of flour.

In addition to being a stop for emigrants, Fort Laramie was also a strong military outpost and became known as the "Guardian of the Trail." Many military expeditions were carried out from Fort Laramie and many treaties signed there. In 1868, Red Cloud and his warriors met with General Sherman at Fort Laramie; the result was the famous treaty in which Red Cloud promised peace.

Fort Laramie was abandoned in the 1880s when it had outlived its usefulness. The westward emigration of covered wagons was over, and the government was no longer waging a military war against the Indians. Today Fort Laramie is a National Historic Site and its yards and buildings are filled with tourists rather than emigrants.

IN THE DAYS OF THE TRAILBLAZERS

1540	Coronado travels north from New Spain (Mexico) to the area that is now part of Kansas.
1620	The Pilgrims land at Plymouth Rock.
1670	The British form the Hudson's Bay Company.
1774	Juan Bautista de Anza travels overland from Mexico to California.
1776	The American colonies declare their independence from Britain.
1778	James Cook sails to the Pacific Northwest.
1779	North-West Company is established by the British.
1792	Robert Gray discovers the mouth of the Columbia River; George Vancouver discovers Vancouver Island.
1793	Alexander Mackenzie leads a cross-continental expedition from the East to the West Coast through Canada.
1803	President Jefferson signs the Louisiana Purchase.
1804-1806	Lewis and Clark make their historic expedition from St. Louis to the Pacific and back again.
1806-1807	Zebulon Pike explores the southern part of the Louisiana Purchase from the Rockies into Spanish Territory and is captured and escorted home.
1807	Manuel Lisa forms a fur trading company in St. Louis.
1807-1808	John Colter explores the Rockies alone and becomes the first white man to see Old Faithful and other wonders of Yellowstone Park.
1810-1811	John Jacob Astor forms the Pacific Fur Company and sends out two parties: one by sea on the *Tonquin*, and one by land led by William Price Hunt.
1812	The U.S. and Great Britain declare war; Robert Stuart discovers South Pass.
1813	Pacific Fur Company is sold to North-West Company.
1819-1820	Stephen H. Long leads an expedition into the Rockies and reports back that the land is uninhabitable; he climbs Pike's Peak.
1821	Mexico gains independence from Spain.
1825	Jim Bridger finds the Great Salt Lake.
1827	Jedediah Smith reaches California via a southern route.
1833	Joe Walker leads an expedition from Green River to California and back and discovers Walker's Pass through the Sierras.
1841	First covered wagon train sets out along the Oregon Trail.
1846	The U.S. declares war on Mexico. General Kearny takes possession of Santa Fe.
1846-1847	The Mormons journey from Nauvoo, Illinois, to the Great Salt Lake to begin a new community.
1848	Gold is discovered in California, beginning the great push westward.